Aromathera

Essential Oils & Aromatherapy

The Ultimate Guide to Improve Health, Reduce Pain and Lose Weight

Introduction

I want to thank you and congratulate you for downloading the book, *"Aromatherapy: Essential oils & Aromatherapy - The Ultimate Guide to Improve Health, Reduce Pain, and Lose Weight."*

How do you feel when you pass outside a bakery and smell the aroma of freshly baked pastries? Most of us, just want to take a moment and savor the scent and in that moment, it just feels so calming. This clearly shows that scent plays a huge role in our physical and mental well-being. This is where the use of essential oils comes in.

Owing to the potent properties of essential oils, these oils are being used to treat depression, anxiety, stress, pain, skin conditions and sleep problems among other things. If you have heard about the amazing power of essential oils and aromatherapy and are not sure how to use essential oils, then this is the right guide for you.

This book will go into depth explaining what essential oils are, how to use them, their benefits as well as various health and mental problems that you can treat easily by simply using essential oils. You will also learn how to make essential oil blends to enjoy the most benefits from essential oils.

Thanks again for downloading this book. I hope you enjoy it!

Table of Contents

Aromatherapy Explained

Also known as Essential Oil therapy, aromatherapy is the practice of using natural oils extracted from various parts of plants to improve physical and psychological wellbeing. Simply put, aromatherapy seeks to unify your physical, psychological, and spiritual processes to enhance your body's healing process.

The word "aroma" implies the application of natural oils though inhalation to trigger various sensations in the body. While inhalation is an ideal way to use these oils, massaging them onto your body, adding them to your bath water and using them orally (for some varieties of oils) are also acceptable ways of using the oils and deriving their benefits. Due to the effectiveness of natural oils, aromatherapy is an alternative treatment for stress, pain, chronic infections, and weight loss.

Oils used in aromatherapy are widely referred to as essential oils; essential oils come from the leaves, roots, barks, stems, seeds, flowers, and other parts of plants. Specific natural oils have distinct active ingredients that make them useful for a particular purpose. For instance, some oils are effective for physical treatment of problems like acne, swelling, and common fungal infections. Other essential oils such as orange blossom oil are very effective at emotional healing since they relax a troubled mind.

Essential oils are what make the concept of aromatherapy work. As we shall see later, these oils have various benefits. Before we look at how to use essential oils in our day-to-day lives, let us look at how aromatherapy actually works.

How Aromatherapy Works

Aromatherapy is, in essence, the use of essential oils for spiritual, emotional, and physical healing. It is important to note that essential oils are generally non-water based phytochemicals constituted of aromatic compounds. They do not contain the fatty acids or lipids found in vegetable and animal oils; however, they are fat-soluble. In addition, they are clean, crisp to touch, and quickly absorbed by the skin; this very nature makes them very efficient.

Since time immemorial, man has used these oils for different healing practices. Since we are a science driven civilization, the question you may be asking is whether science has investigated and approved the use of essential oils as beneficial to the human body.

Although current research is yet to prove how essential oils and aromatherapy actually work, many experts agree: _smells significantly influence the brain._ When you inhale essential oils, the receptors in your nasal area interact with the hippocampus and amygdala, the brain regions that control memories and emotions.

Once the active ingredients present in essential oils reach your brain, scientists believe they stimulate the mental, emotional, and physiological aspects of the brain. Scientists suggest that an essential oil such as lavender has the ability to stimulate brain cells located in the amygdala in a manner similar to what occurs after the use of sedatives. The molecules in different essential oils also interact with enzymes and hormones to alter bodily processes.

The main reason why essential oils are applicable in aromatherapy is their ability to enhance physical and psychological well-being. Essential oils have many applications such as boosting memory or concentration, fighting allergies, stress relief, among other benefits.

Let us examine the specific benefits you stand to enjoy from adopting aromatherapy.

Aromatherapy And Essential Oils: The Key Benefits

Since aromatherapy is a form of therapy, you stand to benefit from a relaxed mind, body, and soul. Aromatherapy is popular for various applications such as weight loss, boosting cognitive function, enhancing mood, and relieving pains such as headaches. These benefits come from the healing properties possessed by essential oils when used as forms of alternative medicine.

Different essential oils possess healing and therapeutic qualities that make them suitable at improving digestion, healing ailments, helping you relax, and to have restful sleep.

Let us discuss how essential oils and aromatherapy practice in general can benefit you:

Pain Relief

It is a common thing to experience occasional or chronic pains such as back pain, joint and muscle pains, swelling and arthritis. You will be surprised to know that essential oils are great at easing pain.

Essential oils such as peppermint, tea tree, lavender, and eucalyptus can ease mild or chronic pain, and provide relief from inflammation or injuries. Essential oils and aromatherapy works well for most pain-related applications. For instance, if you are a woman, you can use essential oils such as frankincense and wintergreen as a home remedy to relieve menstrual pains.

In addition, essential oils such as sandalwood rosemary, eucalyptus, and peppermint are ideal remedies for chronic pains like headaches and migraines. To use these oils, you can mix them with few drops of carrier oils and then massage the blend on your scalp, skin, temples, and the neck.

In addition to relieving pains such as headaches and back pains, essential oils also treat underlying conditions behind occasional pains, conditions such as stress and anxiety. If you did not know, there is a strong link *(http://inspiyr.com/chronic-pain-and-anxiety)* between pain and mood related disorders.

Stress & Anxiety Relief

When applied through body massage, inhalation, or in a refreshing bath, essential oils such as chamomile and oregano can enhance your mood. One study *(http://www.ncbi.nlm.nih.gov/pubmed/21854199)* concluded that patients suffering from stress-related mood disorders felt lesser pain and reduced stress levels after using aromatherapy compared to those who did not use the practice. Another research study *(http://www.ncbi.nlm.nih.gov/pubmed/19216657)* determined that citrus oil and other strong aromas stimulate the brain in a manner that eases depression. Further, cancer patients who adopt aromatherapy can easily manage stress levels and efficiently respond to treatment.

Aromatherapy is ideal as a remedy for mood disorders because it does not have the side effects common with the use of pharmaceutical antidepressants. The power to ease mood disorders comes from the therapeutic scents and other aromatic compounds present in essential oils. These scents and aromatic compounds positively affect cognitive functionality.

Boosts Memory and Sleep

Inability to form short-term memory or total memory loss is a common condition that affects people of different age brackets. For instance, the medical fraternity considers diseases such as Alzheimer's disease and other fatal brain-related disorders incurable. Aromatherapy has the ability to offer relief and slow the progression of Alzheimer's and dementia diseases.

Even in infants and younger patients, aromatherapy boosts memory capacity for a considerable time after treatment. Oils such as sage are ideal for restoring memory and treating brain disorders.

Aromatherapy can also help realign your Circadian rhythms to facilitate restful sleep. Essential oils such as jasmine, chamomile, lavender, rose, and sweet marjoram help you sleep easily and deeply, and wake up energized.

Controls Blood Pressure

Essential oils can manage blood pressure *(http://www.ncbi.nlm.nih.gov/pubmed/17211115)* in a couple of ways. When you massage or breathe in the essentials oils, the body absorbs the relaxing scents, which relieves symptoms of low or high blood pressure.

To understand this fully, understand that the largest blood vessels known as arteries control the flow of blood to all the organs and muscles in the body. As blood pushes against the arterial walls, it creates pressure referred to as blood pressure. The opening and closing of the arteries is what affects blood pressure thus resulting in high or low blood pressure.

If you are suffering from high blood pressure or hypertension, the muscles in your arteries have to push harder, which makes them grow bigger and thicker too. As the arteries thicken, the thickening reduces space for blood flow, which further worsens the high blood pressure condition. So, how does aromatherapy help?

Based on the type of essential oil you adopt, the effect causes the blood vessels to expand or constrict thereby helping manage the blood pressure.

Note: When using essential oils for blood pressure reduction purposes, be mindful of the dosage because some essential oils can worsen high blood pressure symptoms. To be on the safe side, moderate the usage of thyme, rosemary, hyssop, and sage essential oils because these oils contain various stimulants.

For Healing and Recovery

Due to their stimulating properties, essentials oils can boost healing and recovery. Specific essential oils can boost oxygen supply and blood flow to internal organs and wounds especially if you are suffering from internal injuries or recovering from surgery.

Oils like rosehip, buckthorn, calendula, and lavender have anti-microbial properties that help keep your organs protected during the delicate healing processes. In addition, these oils can minimize the discomfort and severity of skin conditions such as eczema and psoriasis.

Improves Hormonal Balance

The body can use effective compounds in essential oils to boost the synthesis of hormones and enzymes required for various metabolic functions. For instance, essential oils such as Clary sage can boost the production of estrogen. Other essential oils such as Ginger and Roman Chamomile improve digestion and production of digestive enzymes.

You can also use oils like peppermint and eucalyptus to destroy bacteria, fungi, and fungal infections. In so doing, you can restore hormonal balance and boost your immune system. Further, a few essential oils boast of estrogenic properties called phytoestrogens; thus, they can effectively control the secretion of hormones.

Important Note: Up to this point, you have learnt that essential oils can add great value to your life. However, be aware that if not administered in right doses or manner, most essential oils are very strong and can cause a number of side effects.

For this reason, when using essential oils, you have to follow certain guidelines to avoid any complications. One rule is to avoid directly applying undiluted essential oils onto the skin because their high concentration can cause skin irritation and inflammation. Secondly, before use, dilute all essential oils in carrier oils such as almond, avocado, jojoba, or olive oils.

Before we discuss carrier oils and their importance, let us first discuss how to use essential oils.

How To Use Essential Oils

In places like hospitals, spas, meditation sessions, and other settings, aromatherapy is a widely applied concept used to offer various benefits. As stated earlier, various essential oils have specified uses such as pain relief, boosting your mood, treating skin conditions, and offering a great sense of relaxation.

Essential oils such as lavender, sandalwood, lemon, rose, and orange are ideal for stress, depression, and anxiety relief. For instance, a blend of frankincense, lavender, and rose oil essential oils is suitable for anxiety especially for pregnant women. This blend can also relieve birth pain and fight the nausea and vomiting that normally occurs during pregnancy.

Nevertheless, to benefit from essential oils, you need to adopt various application techniques such as breathing through a vaporizer or a piece of clothing. You can also use oils in form of sprays or have a professional aromatherapist or close friend massage diluted oils on various trigger points on your body.

An easier way to use essential oils is to add diluted oils to your bath water. This way, you will inhale the aroma, and your skin shall absorb the essential components as you soak in the bath.

Let us discuss the application of various essential oils and explain the reasoning behind each method of application:

Inhalation

This process involves breathing in the essential oils from different modes of application. For instance, you can apply a few drops of desired oil onto a handkerchief, position it near your nose, and then take 4-6 deep breaths of the diffused oil. You can also rub 1-2 drops of essential oils such as lavender into your palms and place your palms near your nose.

You can also heat water in a small bowl, add a few drops of your favorite essential oils, and then breathe in the generated stream for about 5-10 minutes. Alternatively, you can inhale fumes from an essential oil burner or use a diffuser to diffuse the essential oils into the entire room. For this, add a few of drops of essential oils such as spearmint or peppermint into your diffuser according to the package directions. To make essential oils more effective, make various blends using different essential oils with a few drops of carrier oils like jojoba or almond oil.

Topical Massage

You can blend essential oils or mix them with other medications to offer immense benefits for condition such as stress and depression. As stated before, the scents from various oils stimulate positive emotions in the brain enabling you to relax.

In massage therapy, you can also combine different oils into a healing blend and massage the blend onto the forehead, the temples, or the back of the head. Once you have rubbed the essential oil blend onto your body organs or the entire body, allow the oil to sit on your body for about 10-15 minutes for the oils to soak and act on your skin.

Always dilute natural oils in carrier oils such as grape-seed, soya, almond, and olive oils. This is important because dilution helps distribute the oils throughout your body. By so doing, the chances of a negative skin reaction are reduced.

Aroma-Therapeutic Bath

Bathing is a day-to-day activity; therefore, incorporating aromatherapy into your bath routine is not overly complex. To do so, simply add the essential oil of choice to your bath to revitalize your skin. Add 5-10 drops of essential oil or essential oil blend into a warm bathtub (dilute the essential oil/blend in a tablespoon of a carrier).

Warm water (NOT HOT) is ideal because it has heat energy that creates vapors you can inhale as the oils soak into your skin. For better results, avoid adding oils to running water because this may cause evaporation, which will reduce efficiency.

Cold Compress

This method of essential oil application is ideal for women especially in cases of headaches and other pains that accompany the menstruation period. Simply add around 5 drops of your essential oil or blend into 1-quart icy or very cold water, soak a cloth or cotton ball into the bowl, and place it at the back of the neck, stomach, muscles, or onto your forehead.

Creams/Lotions /Salves

To prepare a salve, you need to combine melted beeswax, essential oils, and other substances such as vitamin E, glycerin, and lanolin if desired.

Try the melted form of bees wax and warm bees wax in a ratio of five parts essential oil to 1 part beeswax. It is advisable to add components such as vitamin E that is beneficial to skin especially for topical application and can help preserve your product. Other optional additives such as lanolin can make your salve creamier.

Note: As you have learnt, there are different ways to apply essential oils onto your body to realize their benefits. How to apply any essential oil is dependent on the type of oil used and the results you seek. Some oils are more effective when applied topically on specific areas of your body, while some oils are more effective when directly inhaled into the lungs.

Remember that a majority of essential oils tend to be very strong and concentrated; thus, before directly applying essential oils to the skin, you need to dilute them.

This is where carrier oils come in!

About Carrier Oils

Carrier oils are oils used to dilute essential oils to avert possible side effects such as skin irritation or respiratory problems that may occur after inhalation. While diluting is necessary, the percentage of dilution depends on the type of essential oil, or the condition of the user.

For most adults, a 2 percent dilution with carrier oil is the recommendation. On the other hand, pregnant women and children should adopt 1 percent dilution. A simple way to follow these percentages is to add 1-2 drops of essential oil to 50 drops of carrier oil.

Below are some carrier oils you can use:

* Carrot seed oil

* Sweet almond

* Avocado oil

* Coconut oil

* Extra virgin olive

* Apricot kernel oil

* Jojoba oil

That said, not all carrier oils meet the ideal quality threshold. For this reason, buy unrefined oils or the cold pressed variety. Unrefined carrier oils are of a high quality because they possess most fatty acids, vitamins, and nutrients. These include unrefined olive, jojoba, avocado and carrot seed oils, among others.

In other cases, you can consider buying cold pressed carrier oils. Cold pressed oils are made when vegetable oils are pressed through a machine at a temperature of 120 degrees Fahrenheit. Although cold pressed oils are still considered 'natural', if you go for this option, ensure the oils are RAW because this is the best quality.

Equipped with that information, the only thing you need to know now is which essential oils to use and which oils can make an effective blend. In the following section, we shall discuss specific oils recommended for various conditions and what makes them special.

Adopting Aromatherapy For Optimal Health

Like carrier oils, essential oils also come in different forms or grades based on the concentration or level of processing. Although you may not know much about grading, when deciding which essential oils to use, the rule of thumb is to select only 100% pure therapeutic grade oils. These oils meet the required distillation standards and do not include solvents such as water or other filler oils.

To follow this rule, ensure you properly read labels bearing in mind most companies list down all ingredients used. From labels, you can easily differentiate between pure oils and blends based on the list of constituents.

As stated earlier, each essential oil has specific features that make it ideal as a treatment for particular conditions. Thus, essential oils are easily classifiable into various categories based on their potency, as we shall discuss below.

Let us kick start this section by looking at oils suited for pain relief:

Essential Oils Ideal For Pain Relief

The following essential oils are the most commonly used for pain relief:

Peppermint

This oil has the ability to relieve stress-related headaches. Peppermint has the capacity to lower the intensity of headaches or migraines to the same extent as 1,000 mg of acetaminophen.

The great thing is that this oil has no adverse side effects and can help eliminate the brain fog that normally accompanies headaches or migraines. The ideal way to use this oil is through a head massage.

Clary Sage

Clary sage essential oil is ideal as a pain relief remedy because it produces a narcotic like high sensation effective on most types of pains. If you are a woman, you can use it to reduce pain caused by menstrual cramps and as a tonic to your uterine lining.

In other cases, you can also use clary sage essential oil to treat pains caused by stress and anxiety. To make the oil work for you, ensure you do not take alcohol before, during, or after massaging the oil onto your skin or inhaling it.

Eucalyptus

The most common way to use eucalyptus essential oil is topical application because the oil has strong analgesic and anti-inflammatory properties that destroy organisms that cause skin infections.

Eucalyptus essential oil is also a popular treatment for various problems that cause pain; these include muscular aches and pain, strains, sprains, and nerve pains. When it comes to application, you can use it in cream or lotion forms where you simply rub the oil on the pain affected areas.

To increase the potency of eucalyptus essential oil, dilute it in carrier oil of choice, add a few drops of lavender, and then carefully massage the blend onto the painful or swollen areas. Because eucalyptus is toxic if used in high concentration or large amounts, you only need 2-3 drops of the essential oil.

Wintergreen

Recommended as a viable pain reliever, wintergreen essential oil contains methyl salicylate, a sweet smelling substance that relieves strong pains. After absorption into body cells, the body synthesizes this active compound in a manner that helps the body relieve muscle pains resulting from injuries or inflammation of body tissues.

Due to its strong potency, directly apply the oil on the pain-afflicted regions or areas that experience muscle spasm including along the spine. The recommendation is to use wintergreen oil 2-4 times a day depending on the intensity of the pain.

Essential Oils To Improve Health

Essential oils can treat many health conditions ranging from skin diseases, hypertension, mood disorders, allergies, etc.

In this subsection, we shall simply highlight a few therapeutic oils you can use to treat common health problems:

Ylang Ylang

This oil is effective at fighting mood disorders and improving focus. The reason behind its potency is the sedative properties it stimulates in the brain. The belief is that Ylang Ylang essential oil can help lower your pulse rate and high blood pressure symptoms. In most cases, such symptoms are to blame for mood disorders such as attention deficit disorder (ADD).

You can massage the essential oil on the skin; however, the most effective way to apply this essential oil is through inhalation because when inhaled, the oil easily penetrates the brain barrier, thus boosting attentiveness and easing stress.

By simply inhaling its aroma, you can also improve blood circulation especially if you are suffering from low blood pressure. Alternatively, you can topically apply it on your back, wrists, neck, or feet for similar effects.

Eucalyptus

This essential oil is an effective remedy for many skin conditions such as acne and eczema. Eucalyptus also curbs the contagious tuberculosis disease. Due to presence of active ingredients such as citronellol, linalool, and eucalyptol in the oil, eucalyptus essential oil effectively controls the spread of TB infection by 90 percent.

Eucalyptus oil is most efficient when inhaled by tuberculosis patients. To use the oil, simply dilute 1 part eucalyptus oil in 4 parts vegetable oil and then apply around 1-2 drops onto the chest region.

Apart from the chest, you can also target the chakras located on different regions of the body or diffuse in a handkerchief or diffuser.

Sweet Marjoram

The first thing you will notice about sweet marjoram essential oil is the warm, spicy, and sweet smell; this makes it suitable for inhalation. This oil has high amounts of active ingredients called monoterpenols. These active ingredients have a warming and uplifting effect on the brain.

For this reason, sweet marjoram is particularly effective at strengthening and relaxing the brain to help calm a troubled mind. Inhaling the oil can also reduce obsessive thinking or emotional cravings that cause depression and other mood disorders.

The oil is also effective at reducing nervous exhaustion and chronic lethargy associated with hypertension.

Essential Oils for Healthy Weight Loss

When it comes to weight loss, essential oils do not necessarily help you burn fat; however, what most essential oils do is promote satiety or fullness and curb unnecessary cravings. Other oils may help reduce water retention attributed to weight gain, boost digestion, and prevent bloating.

Let us see which oils and work to facilitate weight loss:

Cinnamon-Bark

Extracted from the bark of cinnamon herb, this oil promotes feelings of satiety long after meals, which helps prevent excessive eating that triggers weight gain. Cinnamon also helps break down sugar for easier absorption into your body, which prevents storage of excess glucose as body fat. In the long term, this can help reduce the level of fatty acids in body tissues and in so doing, trim off excess body fat.

Furthermore, cinnamon essential oil can boost metabolism, improve your gut health, and increase the good bacteria that facilitates weight loss. The oil also has potency to fight Candida that also plays a big role in causing weight gain.

To use the essential oil, simply add 2-3 drops of cinnamon essential oil into honey and warm water and then drink the concoction during breakfast or at night, 1 hour before bedtime. If inhaling is your thing, you can inhale the essential oil fumes from a diffuser before eating or inhale from your drinking water to suppress your appetite. For efficient appetite control, use the oil 30-60 minutes before meals.

Peppermint

Although no firm evidence supports claims that the oil actually works for weight loss, experts agree that peppermint greatly influences your metabolism. In addition, peppermint essential oil aids in healthy weight loss *(https://www.leaf.tv/articles/essential-oils-for-weight-loss)* by treating stomach upsets, indigestion, and inflammation in the GI tract and boosting flow of bile.

The oil also boosts the level of gastric juices, and relieves bloat and gas in the intestines in a bid to improve food metabolisms. To relieve stomach problems and possibly rev up metabolism, dilute 2 drops of peppermint essential oil in 2-3 drops olive or coconut oil and rub onto your stomach. You can also add a drop of peppermint oil to drinking water to treat a stomachache, or look for already made capsules.

Grapefruit

Of all essential oils, this oil works in a manner that directly contributes to weight loss. The oil helps dissolve fat deposits from body tissues, reduce water retention that causes weight gain, and prevents bloating.

Grapefruit essential oil is very effective at weight loss because of the presence of the active ingredient d-limonene, which helps release fatty acids into the blood. The liver then easily breaks down these stored fats to generate fuel or energy for metabolic functions.

Apart from the d-limonene agents, grapefruit oil also has antioxidants such as Lycopene that can help cleanse the lymphatic system and detoxify the body. To derive these benefits, simply add about 1-2 drops to a glass of drinking water and drink it daily preferably during breakfast to help burn fat and flush out toxins that cause weight gain.

Lemon

Like grapefruit essential oil, lemon essential oil contains d-Limonene compound, vitamin C, and other minerals that help fight intestinal parasites that could be the underlying cause of weight gain. Lemon essential oil also helps fight digestive problems, boost your energy levels, and balance the metabolism; this boosts weight loss. Further, lemon essential oil helps the body eliminate toxins stored in fat cells; these toxins greatly contribute to additional weight.

You can use this essential oil in a number of ways such as inhaling preferably from an inhaler, or simply adding 1-2 drops to drinking water. Due to its high rate of skin permeability, you can also massage it on the areas with cellulite to facilitate the thinning of fat cells.

Blends And Essential Oil Recipes

The concept behind essential oil blending is to increase potency of oils and their ability to cure physical and mental conditions. The practice of blending is not complicated if you understand the aroma profiles of the essential oils you need to use.

Particular oils have different aromas that change when exposed to air or blended with other oils. Therefore, when blending, take care not to expose oils to air and try to make a blend with a strong aroma profile to achieve maximum benefits.

To create blends, the first thing you need to do is determine the aroma profiles of the oils you intend to use. To do so, dispense a drop of oil onto unscented tissue. Your aim here is to inhale the concentrated oil and decide how the oil profile changes with exposure to air.

From the impression, or the descriptive image you build from these oils, you can then figure out how they can work together. You do not need to learn rocket science for this; the idea is to create an effective blend. Remember, you can create as many blends as you can manage.

Here are a few essential oil blends to get you started:

Tea Tree Blend

This blend is effective for skin conditions such as acne, a condition caused by overproduction of sebum, or hormonal imbalance.

This blend is ideal because both lavender and tea tree oils contain antiseptic properties that help kill bacteria responsible for skin infections.

To create this blend, mix the following oils:

1 drop tea tree

1 drop Lavender

1 drop geranium or German chamomile

50 drops of carrier oil such as jojoba

To use, clean the spot or infected region, and then sparingly apply diluted oil using a cotton pad. It is good to apply the blend every night until the acne or skin patches fully disappear.

The Soothing Blend

This blend is ideal for pain relief because of potency of oils used to make it.

To make your blend, combine the following:

2-3 drops of Marjoram

2-3 drops of White fir

Some Epsom salt

2 drops coconut oil as carrier oil

For pain relief, simply massage the blend onto the forehead, the temples, or the back of the head. Remember, you are free to decide the dilution level based on your skin reactivity.

Hypertension Blend

To treat high blood pressure, combine the oils listed below and then massage a few drops over the heart region and major blood vessels.

3 drops Ylang Ylang

6 drops each of Clary sage, Marjoram, and lavender

30-ml of carrier oil such as almond

Weight Loss Blend

This blend addresses metabolism-related issues such as nausea and indigestion. To prepare the blend, combine oils in a non-reactive bowl and then gently massage the blend onto your stomach. You can use cotton or another suitable cloth to do it in a clockwise direction. Combine:

4 drops of ginger

3 drops of peppermint

4 drops lavender

Insomnia Blend

This blend treats hormonal disturbances that cause lack of sleep, headaches, dizziness, depression, as well as chronic agitation. Combine the oils and massage the blend on the skin or alternatively, add 2 teaspoons of the blend into your bath water.

15 drops of bergamot

10 drops of lavender

4 ounces of vegetable oil

2 drops of Ylang Ylang

3 drops of frankincense

10 drops of sandalwood

This particular blend is effective when directly inhaled. You can also omit the vegetable oil and pour the mixture onto a simmering pan of water. Breathe in the fumes before going to bed until your sleeping patterns improve.

Bonus: Effective Essential Oil Use

Adhering to the following tips and tricks will ensure the effectiveness of essential oils once you use them (as well as your safety as you use the oils):

Dilute essential oils in carrier oils

This is a must-do for most if not all essential oils. Failure to dilute essential oils can lead to severe negative reactions such as skin burn or skin cancer. To dilute natural oils, use vegetable oils such as sweet almond oil or other carrier oils.

To determine the dilution level, you can perform a skin patch test by first applying a little diluted amount onto your skin. Then check whether you experience any adverse reaction. If you don't then use that dilution ratio.

Don't expose essential oils to air

As stated before, essential oils are volatile and can lose their aroma profiles when exposed to air. Store them in dark-colored bottles away from light or heat sources.

Apply oils as described

Only a few citrus oils are okay to ingest or take orally; therefore, never eat or ingest essential oils unless otherwise instructed by a medical practitioner. When massaging essential oils onto your body, avoid application near the eyes or mucus membranes; this will prevent possible negative reactions,

During pregnancy, avoid aromatherapy

If you are pregnant, avoid essential oils such as thyme, rosemary, rose, peppermint, myrrh, marjoram, sweet fennel, wintergreen, hyssop, clove bud, basil, and bitter almond. These can affect you or the unborn baby.

Conclusion

Thank you again for downloading this book!

I hope you have learnt about essential oils and aromatherapy and now have the adequate knowledge to use essential oils properly and enjoy the amazing benefits these oils offer. As a point of caution, always seek the advice of your doctor before using essential oils. This is because essential oils can interfere with your medication or present health condition. For instance, oils such as thyme, sage, rosemary, or hyssop can worsen high blood pressure symptoms. Further, if you suffer from epilepsy, avoid essential oils such as rosemary, sage, hyssop, and sweet fennel to minimize possible problems.

Finally, if you enjoyed this book, would you be kind enough to leave a review for this book on Amazon?

Preview of "Mediterranean Diet - Easy Recipes for A Healthy Diet And Permanent Weight Loss"

The typical western diet is packed full of sugar, salt, and fat and the combination of those three is explosively unhealthy. Obesity is on the rise if you will forgive the pun, so are instances of heart disease, cognitive decline and many other medical conditions and health risks, all associated with our diets.

That is why so many people are turning to The Mediterranean Diet. This is more than just a diet; this is a way of life that is firmly based in traditional Mediterranean foods and drinks. Unlike many other so-called diets, the Mediterranean diet allows you to live your life freely, without restriction. You can join your friends and family for a meal or go to a restaurant without having to worry too much about what you are eating.

The Mediterranean diet brings together the culture and traditions of countries like Greece, Spain, Italy, and France, providing you with a wide variety of foods to choose from. While Mediterranean cuisine varies from country to country and even region to region within a country, it is mostly based on fruit, vegetables, nuts, cereal grains, fish and olive oil, with little meat being consumed.

Mediterranean cuisine varies by region and has a range of definitions, but is largely based on vegetables, fruits, nuts, beans, cereal grains, olive oil, and fish. And let's not forget a good drop of red wine to wash it all down with.

If you are ready to try something that has been around for years, a diet that has been proven time and time again to be the healthiest in the world, then you have come to the right place. You are about to start a new journey; a journey where you train your body to forget about processed foods full of fat and sugar and learn to enjoy foods that are full of essential nutrients, natural foods that take us back to how we used to live.

To check out the rest of "Mediterranean Diet" please search on Amazon for:

"Mediterranean Diet: Easy Recipes for A Healthy Diet And Permanent Weight Loss By Cooking Delicious Meals"

Or go to:

http://amzn.to/2bWSmnX

Printed in Great Britain
by Amazon